THE SUCCESS CODE

FOR

YOUR DREAM RETIREMENT

BY

Peter A. Vaughn

TABLE OF CONTENTS

INTRODUCTION TO KEYS TO SUCCESSFUL RETIREMENT

In recent decades, there has been a significant evolution in the idea of retiring. Retirement has changed from being seen as the far-off culmination of life's journey to becoming an active and dynamic stage when opportunities for growth, exploration, and fulfilment abound. Retirement today signifies not an end but a fresh beginning—a thrilling chapter in a person's life story that can last decades.

The decisions we make and the tactics we use, as we approach retirement, can have a significant impact on the calibre and enjoyment of our post-work years. The goal of this book, "The Success Code for Your Dream Retirement," is to provide you with the knowledge, insights, and tools you need to embrace retirement as a period of significant personal growth and purpose as well as to protect your financial future.

Planning for retirement may be an exciting and intimidating adventure. The notion of giving up a typical career throws up a world of opportunities, including more time for leisure activities, travel, family time, and community involvement. However, it also poses certain difficulties, such as monetary ambiguities, health issues, and the issue of how to make the most of this newfound freedom.

We'll begin a transforming examination of the secrets to a good retirement in the pages that follow. This retirement will be marked by financial security, physical and emotional well-being, meaningful participation, and a legacy that lasts beyond your lifetime. This book is your dependable travel companion whether you are approaching retirement, taking advantage of its perks now, or making long-term plans.

Let's pause for a moment to consider the changing nature of retirement before we get into the specifics of retirement preparation. Retirement no longer equates to idle leisure time or social isolation in the twenty-first century. Instead, it presents a chance for self-reflection, self-awareness, and the pursuit of hobbies that may have been put off for a while.

The prospective length of retirement has greatly increased as life expectancy keeps increasing. What was once thought to be a momentary break after a lifetime of work can now last for several decades. The retirement phase's elongation offers previously unheard-of chances and difficulties.

Today's retirees can start new occupations, travel widely, further their education, get involved in philanthropy, and enjoy full, active lives long into their 80s and beyond. But in order to ensure that one's resources can support a pleasant lifestyle throughout this extended era, careful financial planning is also necessary given the lengthened retirement period.

Furthermore, retirement success now encompasses more than just financial stability. Although it is unquestionably important, financial stability is only one aspect of the puzzle. The ability to leave a lasting legacy, good health, solid social ties, and personal fulfilment are all essential components of a happy retirement. In " The Success Code for Your Dream To help you on your Retirement journey, in "Retirement," we will examine each of these aspects in-depth and provide you with useful advice, doable plans, and examples from real life.

This book is a flexible toolset that may be customised to your particular circumstances and goals rather than a one-size-fits-all prescription.

CHAPTER 1

KEYS TO SUCCESSFUL RETIREMENT PLANNING

The process of planning for retirement involves many steps and changes over time. You must create the financial cushion that will cover everything if you want to retire in luxury, security, and with plenty of fun. Planning your route there is the serious but somewhat boring portion, which is why it makes sense to focus on it.

Thinking about your retirement objectives and how long you have to achieve them is the first step in retirement planning. Then you should consider the several retirement account types that can assist you in raising the funds necessary to finance your future. You must invest the money you save in order for it to grow.

The final aspect of preparing is taxes: If you've accumulated tax deductions for the money you've put into your retirement accounts over the years, you'll face a significant tax charge when you start taking those funds out. While you are saving for the future and after the day comes when you actually stop working, there are strategies to reduce the retirement tax burden.

Retirement planning has changed significantly during the past 30 or 40 years. Actually, your father (or mother) is not retiring. In fact, a lot of individuals aren't even familiar with the term "retirement." It has been called the "second act," "third age," or "retirement" stage of life, as people go from full-time employment to other endeavours. Some respondents to surveys have even said they have no intention of ever retiring.

Planning for retirement is an important task that goes beyond securing your financial future to include more comprehensive aspects of creating a fulfilling retirement.

All of these topics will be covered here. But first, start by studying the measures that all individuals, regardless of age, should take in order to create a sound retirement plan.

Defined benefit (DB) pension schemes were commonplace a few generations ago. Benefits were guaranteed to employees in accordance with a formula depending on their income and number of years of service. The actuarial risk was on the employers to lay away enough money to provide a monthly income stream to employees for life, but average retirements were brief, lasting only approximately 5 years. DB pension arrangements are substantially less prevalent today.

The most popular type of retirement plan in use today is the defined contribution (DC) plan, which includes 401(k) plans and places all investment risk on the employees.

Participants in DC plans must decide whether and how to invest before choosing certain investment items. They will have their accumulated savings and investment returns upon retirement. Unlike DB plans, which offer lifetime income guarantees, DC plans do not. Instead, retirement income is only available while assets are still in existence. Workers are in charge of generating money from their assets. Additionally, today's retirements endure 25 years on average, with a range of up to 40 years (or more), depending on the retiree's age, the health of their families, their own health, and other variables.

All of these themes emphasise the importance of forethought and individual responsibility for a comfortable older life. Ten suggestions are provided below to help you have a successful retirement:

10 Pointers for Effective Retirement Planning

Beginning early

 According to the 4% rule, if someone anticipates having monthly costs of Rs. 1 lakh after retirement, they will need to have a minimum investment corpus of Rs. 3 crores. For many, assembling this sum can take a long time. Therefore, the secret to getting better returns is to start saving and investing early in life. To maximise the corpus, experts advise beginning retirement planning as early as your 20s. By the time retirement arrives, the power of compounding can guarantee that one has enough money to handle inflation.

Set away more money than is necessary.

One can get a good sense of the retirement age and income till retirement based on their current and future job aspirations. This might serve as the starting point for evaluating the amount of money needed to cover costs after retirement. It is preferable to set aside more money than one may actually need when making financial plans. Since many people choose to retire early and overall life expectancy has increased, leading to a longer retirement period, this will aid in avoiding any financial burden later in life.

The 4% principle

It's important to monitor the potential income an investment could produce when planning for retirement. The 4 per cent rule can be applied in this situation. This rule states that in order for retirement savings to survive at least 30 years after retirement, a retiree must plan to remove up to 4% of their portfolio each year after retiring. This cautious approach helps to prevent additional withdrawals from the retirement corpus and makes sure that it doesn't run out too soon.

Choose your options for investing and savings carefully.

There are many savings and investing choices available on the market, but selecting one or a few of them might be difficult. For this, one must carefully and completely assess the possibilities that have been narrowed down. Personal risk tolerance and investing horizon are two elements that can help with improved decision-making. For instance, one may design their financial portfolio so that as they get older, they start to focus more on debt and less on equities.

Add real estate to your portfolio.

Owning a property that can provide rental income in retirement is another financial advice to employ for effective retirement planning. A person can generate a bigger rental income if they have more assets. Rents rise annually, so this form of income can help a retiree keep their finances in line with growing inflation. You can also sell a house you acquired when you were younger to raise money for retirement.

Managing debt effectively

It makes sense to pay off debts as soon as possible while making retirement plans. Repaying debt on time helps maintain healthy financial habits and reduces the chance of depleting retirement funds. Dues that go unpaid have high-interest rates and interfere with retirement planning.

Set aside enough money for medical costs

People frequently underestimate the amount of money needed to cover rising medical costs after retirement. Old age can bring about a considerable increase in medical issues, and since healthcare costs are rising, one must make enough preparations in the form of medical insurance and savings. A realistic estimate of the family's financial needs after retirement can be obtained by noting their general health, medical history, genetic problems, and chosen hospitals for treatment.

Consider the financial dependence of the family

The financial needs of family members who might outlive the retiree should be taken into account while making retirement plans. Younger and healthier dependents may live longer than the retiring family member. As a result, when developing a financial plan for retirement, one must ensure that such dependents have enough financial security.

Even when the retiree passes away, a family insurance policy can provide for the financial needs of the dependents.

Track development

No plan is finished unless its progress is tracked and any defects are addressed. As a result, it is crucial to periodically review the retirement plan carefully so that modifications can be made to costs, savings, and assets.

It's crucial to keep in mind that one's financial condition changes over time in this situation. As one gets older, they could transition into occupations paying more or start their own businesses. As a result, both the capacity to save and to invest more money increases.

Don't forget insurance

People who work in the private sector or who own enterprises must obtain enough insurance coverage for themselves and their families because there is little government assistance available for retirement expenses. In addition to the previously mentioned health insurance, home and life insurance are equally important for having enough financial security.

CHAPTER 2

WHAT NOT TO DO BEFORE RETIREMENT

You must be forward-thinking and realistic about your objectives if you want to avoid the worst retirement blunders. Sadly, it's too simple to make poor financial decisions when getting ready for retirement. 40% of non-retired Americans believe their retirement savings are on track, according to the Federal Reserve. None of the 60% who believe they are behind schedule, though, undoubtedly didn't want to ruin or underfund their retirement.

Retirement is a major life event for the majority of people. It rivals or exceeds the size of weddings and graduations. Retirement is a stressful time for many people. Making plans in advance can help to reduce some of this stress. What can be prepared for in advance versus what can wait is a dilemma. Everyone will differ on this, but if you're getting ready for retirement, there are some generalisations regarding priorities that may be made.

The idea that retirement marks the end of your working years is a widespread one. In actuality, it may be an opportunity for you to reinvent yourself and spend your free time doing what you've always wanted to do. However, many people make errors prior to retiring that have a detrimental effect on their financial situation once they are retired.

Your daily life will be impacted by your retirement decision in a variety of ways, both personally and financially. Your retirement years should be pleasurable, but in order to fully take advantage of your newfound freedom, it's crucial to make sure your finances are in order.

It's vital to think about what not to do in retirement when you're planning all the enjoyable things you may do with your leisure time because some errors can throw your retirement plans off course.

The following are the 15 things you must avoid:

Taking Social Security Benefits Too Soon

Your Social Security retirement benefit may be commenced as early as age 62 or as late as age 70. People prefer to retire as soon as they can since, as of 2015, around 33% of men and nearly 40% of women were receiving Social Security at age 62. It may be tempting to begin collecting as soon as you are able, but remember that the time you begin collecting will have an impact on the amount of your monthly benefits for the rest of your life.

Even though you may be able to begin receiving benefits at age 62, delaying until your full retirement age, which varies from 65 to 67 depending on the year you were born, results in a monthly payment that is almost 30% greater than you would receive at that age. Your payout will max out and be an additional 32% higher than at full retirement age if you can wait until age 70.

Additionally, if you start receiving Social Security benefits before reaching full retirement age, your payment will be reduced by $1 for every $2 of income earned over the annual cap of $17,040 (for 2018).

As soon as you become eligible, Eric McClain, a certified financial planner with McClain Lovejoy, advises against taking Social Security. Delaying and possibly even using your other assets first may make sense.

The ideal course of action is to keep working as long as you can to maximise your Social Security payments unless you are physically unable to do so.

Not Investing Enough Aggressively

Once you approach retirement age, you could have a tendency to stop actively investing or even sell off all of your current holdings. However, this is not a prudent financial move. Your financial journey does not finish with retirement; rather, it really just begins. A 65-year-old male has a 20% probability of living to age 90, according to the Society of Actuaries (via Vanguard) and a 41% chance of living to age 85. A woman who is 65 years old has a 32% chance of living to age 90 and a 53% chance of living to age 85. If a man and woman are married, there is a higher likelihood that at least one of them will live to a certain age.

You still need to invest a portion of your retirement savings for development because retirement is not the end of your financial life. Depending on a variety of circumstances specific to each retiree's position, you should allocate different portions of your entire portfolio. Being overly cautious can cause you to outlive your retirement savings.

No matter what your individual circumstances are, diversification—which involves investing across all asset classes, including stocks, bonds, real estate trusts, and more—is the key to a successful retirement investment strategy.

Ignoring Inflation's Effects

According to Statista, the inflation rate for 2018 was 2.38 per cent, and over the following few years, it is expected to vary from 2.18 per cent to 2.64 per cent. Even though it may seem insignificant, inflation nevertheless has an impact on how far a dollar will go. This is especially true for money kept in fixed savings accounts, which will depreciate over time unlike money kept in other investments.

Your purchasing power will be halved in 24 years at an inflation rate of 3 per cent, which is about average. Given the aforementioned data and the fact that we are living longer, inflation is the deadliest adversary of any retiree.

What can you do to lessen how inflation affects your retirement savings?

Plan conservatively for inflation while accounting for rising healthcare expenses.

Invest aggressively enough to remain ahead of inflation.

Be ready to alter your expenditures and withdrawals from retirement accounts.

Choosing not to see a financial planner for retirement advice

Many people lack enough financial preparation for retirement, but many are unwilling to take the time to meet with a financial counsellor to learn how to do so.

Both pre-retirees and those who have already retired can benefit from seeking the guidance of a knowledgeable, fee-only financial advisor to keep on track.

Don't let your pride or reluctance to spend the money on an advisor prevent you from getting the advice you need because you only get one chance at retirement.

Consult a financial planning specialist to gain an unbiased outside perspective on your position. Based on your projected resources, such as Social Security, any pensions you may have, tax-deferred retirement savings, and more, he or she can assist you in creating a retirement income strategy.

If you're unsure of how your life will be in retirement, it's best to consider a variety of options, such as staying in your current house or moving, and work out with your adviser how to handle your finances regardless of the decision you choose.

Lack of preparation for medical expenses

Healthcare expenses may be overlooked when calculating the expenditures of living you'll need to pay for in retirement, such as housing and everyday essentials. This is especially true if you are currently in good health and don't need to make any further purchases for medical care.

The best remedy, according to Kiplinger's Retirement Report, is to ensure that your retirement plan accounts for this significant line item and to discover strategies to reduce future costs or create income streams to cover spending.

According to a Fidelity analysis, a couple retiring in 2017 would require $275,000 to cover healthcare expenses in retirement. Even for someone with a nest egg of more than $1 million, this is a considerable sum of money. Social Security will receive a 2 per cent cost-of-living rise for 2018, but many retirees will also see an increase in their Medicare costs.

A health savings account (HSA), for individuals who are still employed and have access to one, can be a terrific method to boost retirement funds and accumulate a nest egg with pre-tax money that can be withdrawn tax-free in retirement for approved medical expenditures.

Make sure your funds can cover healthcare expenses that aren't covered by Medicare if you've previously retired. Remember that you'll need savings to pay for both short-term and long-term medical costs.

Failure to Prepare a Retirement Budget

According to a GOBankingRates analysis, more than 40% of Americans had less than $10,000 saved for retirement. Nearly 33 per cent of soon-to-retire baby boomers reported having less than $10,000 saved for retirement, which was not significantly lower than the overall number. Even if your nest fund makes you feel secure, you should sit down and determine how long your savings will actually endure.

It's crucial to actually take the time to perform the maths to ensure that everything will add up, regardless of how convinced you are that you are in a good place financially to retire.

Making a budget for the lifestyles you want in retirement is an excellent first step for folks who are getting ready to retire. Where will you call home? How will you proceed? How much will it cost each month to support your lifestyle? Do you have the means to support this way of life?

If not, you should reconsider your retirement plans. Maybe you should cut back on your activities or go back to work. A budget enables you to assess your current situation and determine whether you will have enough money in retirement.

The Absence of a Retirement Income Strategy

Many retirees have several sources of income in retirement, but they may not plan ahead for the best methods to use each one of those income sources.

Managing payments from numerous retirement accounts as well as other sources, such as pension or Social Security, is one of the most challenging elements of retirement.

You must make a choice regarding which accounts to tap first and in what order. What effects on taxes does this have? How will Medicare and other benefits be impacted by your income? Without a retirement income strategy, the effects could be disastrous, so prepare for the worst by starting now.

Not Accounting for Taxes' Effect on Retirement

It can be simple to forget about all the taxes you still owe in retirement after you aren't receiving a pay check from which taxes are automatically withheld, including property taxes and income taxes on retirement income. Additionally, you want to ensure that you're utilising all opportunities to reduce your taxes in retirement.

Taxes may play a significant role in retirement. Retirement account withdrawals, including those from IRAs and 401(k)s, are often fully taxable at ordinary income rates. Depending on your income, Social Security may also be taxable. These withdrawals are also added to any other income you may have.

Although most pension payments are taxable, some pensions may not be subject to state income taxes.

Likewise, annuities are taxed. If the money received from a non-qualified annuity (bought outside of an IRA or retirement account) is less than the principal amount you contributed, taxes will apply.

However, provided all regulations are met, a Roth IRA is not taxed, and a Roth 401k can be rolled into a Roth IRA to receive a similar benefit.

The bottom line is that retirees need to account for taxes. There may be possibilities for where to get money in various circumstances, and it's crucial to take taxes into account while making any such choices

A Home Sold Too Soon

If your property is your biggest asset, you might be ready to sell it as soon as you retire so you can use the proceeds to boost your nest fund.

Before listing your house for sale, it's crucial to take into account the housing market where you live. If you live in a city where home prices are exploding, it makes sense to sell your property, but if you live in a place where home values are falling, it is not a smart financial move. According to a 2017 GOBankingRates research, home prices had dropped $5,000 or more in some locations in the South and Southeast, particularly Texas.

If you reside in a location where home values are declining, instead of selling your current property immediately, think about using it to generate more income. While you try out living in a new place, rent your home to tenants for a year. That achieves two goals. With that answer, you can test out a different location to see if you'd like to live there. Additionally, you make enough money to cover your housing costs while allowing your local real estate market time to recover.

Making Uncontrolled Purchases

Whether you end up overpaying on trips, golf memberships, home improvements, or any other luxury that you want to be able to enjoy with your new free time, it's easy to get caught up in a spending frenzy once you retire.

Your retirement funds may be depleted more quickly than you expect if you spend money that you haven't prepared for.

Include "fun" costs in your long-term retirement budget, such as money for inexpensive holidays and money to indulge in hobbies.

If you discover that a pastime or trip requires more money than you had originally budgeted, consider strategies to balance your expenditure by making savings elsewhere, such as by eating out less the following month. Alternatively, think about selling an item you no longer require.

Not utilising discounts for seniors

Many locations, including theme parks, movie theatres, and restaurants, give seniors discounts. Your discount may increase if you are an AARP or AMAC member.

However, many individuals fail to consider taking advantage of elder discounts and "early bird specials," either because they are unaware of the availability of such offers or as a matter of pride.

Simply speaking, declining a discount entails losing out on money. If the opportunity presents itself, you should seize it. If you do, you might discover that you have extra cash to spend on other things.

Ask whether a discount is available if you're hesitant; the worst they can say is no, right? You really don't have an excuse not to take advantage of a deal or a coupon, especially because websites like The Senior List make it simple to find ways to save by providing detailed listings of deals each year. Even just from their list of restaurants, you may save an incredible 25%. Not just entertainment can be cut back on; consider the costs of your monthly budget-busting medications, roadside assistance, cell phone, and internet service.

Abusing Your Grandchildren

It goes without saying that you adore your grandchildren and want every moment spent with them to be memorable. However, sometimes this entails adopting a full-on fairy godparents attitude and stocking the toy aisle, or giving kids to activities that are more expensive than your finances can actually support. Spend some time using these apps to teach your grandchildren about money.

Plan your time wisely instead of sprinkling fairy dust and fulfilling all of your children's wishes; many activities are free. Children frequently get free admission to museums with engaging interactive exhibits and shows. Visit a nearby playground or go for a walk in the park; alternatively, borrow fresh books from the library.

Consider crafting a DIY craft or preparing a meal or dessert together that costs considerably less than a store-bought toy or a meal out if you want something tangible to show for your time spent together.

Keeping your second car in the garage

Many retirees still make the error of holding onto their second car even when they no longer travel frequently or largely rely on public transportation, which is usually available at a subsidised rate.

After having two cars for so long, you may simply be unable to imagine downsizing, or there may be some other factor keeping you from getting rid of that extra set of needless wheels.

Parking a car in your driveway that you don't use is equivalent to leaving a large bag of cash unopened. It's a waste if you're not using it.

Keeping a second car takes up room that could be used for something else, and it loses value every day you leave it parked. This means that if you don't use it, you are actually losing money instead of just leaving it on the table.

If you think you can afford it, think about selling your car. One vehicle (or none) may force you to adopt better habits, such as increasing your walking and cutting down on unnecessary travel, which will lower your expenses and carbon impact. Additionally, you'll avoid spending the money you do now on maintenance and insurance.

Investing in Scams

Everyone appears to come out of the woodwork to ask you for money after you retire. Even when some goods and services are no longer necessary in retirement, it is simple to be persuaded to buy by a fast-talking salesperson.

For instance, people frequently end up spending money on investments and insurance products without having any real need to. Sometimes it might be challenging to even recognise that you are being scammed.

Some of these are extra services that you don't need, while others are outright frauds. You must first be aware of what you already possess in order to prevent being pressured into paying for something you don't need or want.

Examine your insurance policies to see what they now cover — possibly with the help of a financial counsellor if you're still unsure. Never purchase additional insurance policies, annuities, or other financial products without carefully reviewing them; if necessary, get the help of a relative, attorney, or financial expert to analyse the paperwork. Too frequently, con artists target senior citizens.

Failing to do the maths A Major Life Event Later

Most people wish to quit doing maths when they retire in order to concentrate on relaxing. They put in so much effort and sacrifice to get there that they might not understand the need to maintain a close check on their finances now that they have succeeded.

Large medical expenses, a spouse's death, or a divorce - yes, it occurs after 65 — are all signs that it's time to reevaluate.

You risk running out of money earlier than anticipated if you don't periodically review your finances, particularly after a life-changing event. If you have to support two houses instead of one after a divorce, it might be difficult to maintain your lifestyle, especially in retirement. Additionally, you need to think about how retirement savings will be divided.

A spouse's death also results in altered financial situations. For any lost income, surviving spouses will need to make a new budget. To determine how spending and income may vary in retirement, consult a financial advisor. If you receive a life insurance payout or other benefits, consult your counsellor to determine the best method to invest, save, or pay off debt with the money you receive.

CHAPTER 3

HOW TO HAVE A SUCCESSFUL RETIREMENT

Although retirement planning may seem overwhelming, concentrating on the degree of power you actually have over key issues might help you feel more in charge. Market returns, future tax laws, and legislative and regulatory changes are some variables beyond your control. We discuss seven key retirement planning principles using slides from the Guide to Retirement, giving investors the assurance to make better-educated choices and take proactive measures towards a successful retirement.

Have you ever looked at someone who is enjoying retirement and wondered, "What the hell did they do to get there?" When they talk about their aspirations to tour the world or to be obscenely charitable, they do so with glee in their voices. And it spreads easily!

So how did they accomplish it? First of all, they have likely been retirement-smart rather than financial whizzes. They didn't possess a special recipe for a successful retirement. They also didn't maintain incredibly intricate portfolios or constantly monitor the stock market.

Ready to learn what they did, then? It will astound you. Learn this: Year after year, they contribute money to their retirement accounts on a monthly basis. Gasp! They controlled their spending and put an emphasis on saving. Along the way, they also had assistance from a seasoned investor. I'm done now! Not really that difficult. It's doable by anyone.

But how does that manifest itself in real life? Let's look at some strategies for retirement success that anyone can use.

They are aware that their primary asset for accumulating wealth is their income.

The most efficient and dependable approach for wise investors to accumulate wealth is through their income. That is correct! They give every dollar in their household income a purpose, regardless of how much or how little it is. They avoid debt as well because they are aware that doing so provides them the freedom to do more with their money, such as make future plans. How can you save for retirement if you're continuously sending your hard-earned money to the bank? According to The National Study of Millionaires, almost three-quarters of millionaires never carried a credit card balance in their lives.

They establish a monthly budget and follow it.

People who are financially wise are aware of their grocery, dining out, and clothing budgets. Additionally, even if it's just a few dollars, they drive by the coffee shop if they run out of money for coffee before payday in order to stay under their budget. Why? because money grows on trees. They are aware that over time, small, regular decisions have the most impact.

They put 15% of their salary towards retirement.

Smart investors save 15% of their household income for retirement (Baby Step 4) after paying off all of their debts (other than the mortgage) and setting aside three to six months' worth of spending. In fact, 48% of millionaires claimed to save 16% or more of their monthly income!

Dave Ramsey discovered in his most recent book, Baby Steps Millionaires, that those who adhere to the Baby Steps and put 15% of their income into tax-advantaged retirement accounts do it on average in less than 20 years. By investing that sum, they can work towards other crucial financial objectives like saving for their children's college and paying off their mortgage early while still making significant progress towards a secure retirement. Talk about a financial strategy!

They invest with a long-term outlook in mind.

Investment is a marathon, not a sprint, as people who are financially knowledgeable know. Due to the ups and downs in the stock market, they don't switch from one investment to another. They invest with a long-term perspective, which explains why. They are aware that investing in mutual funds with a track record of consistent growth is a wise long-term strategy. So, keep your eyes on the prize and think long-term!

They do not live affluent lives.

Retirement-savvy individuals don't spend more than they earn. Nope! 94% of millionaires, according to The National Study of Millionaires, live below their means. They purchase affordable homes and pay cash for their vehicles and travel. There is still enough money left over to save for retirement.

They don't care about keeping up with the Joneses, thus they don't require the newest and coolest technology. Oh, and did I mention? According to the report, 93% of millionaires also use coupons. They have a keen eye for bargains, are pleased with what they have, and maintain their focus on their financial objectives. All of that assists in helping them maintain their priorities month after month.

They don't interfere with their 401(k) programmes.

This is a major issue. It may seem like a fantastic idea to borrow money from your 401(k) plan in order to cover an urgent unanticipated need. But savvy long-term investors are aware that taking out a 401(k) loan has significant risks, including taxes and penalties if you can't pay the debt back. Even worse, the money you borrow could lose thousands of dollars in long-term compound growth. The final word? Never do it! It's simply not worth it.

Get-rich-quick investments are avoided by them.

People who are committed to funding their retirement goals over the long run don't waste time looking for assets that will make them wealthy quickly. They are wise enough not to follow investing fads that are surrounded by a lot of buzz but have little concrete results to show for it.

People who are financially literate avoid taking significant, unneeded risks with their money. They don't stake everything on a few stocks, and they most certainly don't empty their bank accounts to "invest" in Dogecoin. Instead, they continue to use the investments and tactics that have assisted millions of Americans in building wealth responsibly—and you should do the same.

They have a strategy, which they adjust as necessary.

Good investors are aware of where their money is going and how much it is increasing. They check up with an investing professional once a year to keep track of their money. They also consult with their professional after major life events, such as the birth of a child, a change in employment, or a move of the family, to assess the potential effects on their savings strategy.

We didn't say they monitor their investments every hour on the hour; we just stated they keep an eye on things. Avoid doing it! You'll only wind up driving yourself crazy and become more tempted to make hasty, careless investment judgements. Be persistent and proactive!

If they are married, they collaborate on projects with their partner.

Investment success is more likely for couples that have similar financial values. They decide jointly on their financial goals and how they'll achieve them, and they work together to achieve success. A lot of couples also share a desire to be generous with their money in addition to being concerned about making ends meet.

Hey, you're not off the hook whether you're recently single or single and single! Find an accountability partner who will motivate you and keep you focused on achieving your financial objectives. This person could be a close friend or a family member you can trust. Don't attempt this alone. You need someone rooting for you from your corner!

They have regular meetings with a financial expert.

A skilled specialist is worth their weight in gold, as wise investors are aware. In fact, according to 68% of the millionaires we surveyed for The National Study of Millionaires, they consulted a financial advisor or investing expert to achieve their million-dollar net worth.

It makes a significant difference to have someone on your side to guide you in selecting the appropriate mutual funds. Retirement planning is just too crucial to be done solely on your own, people.

Are you prepared to begin and receive advice from a reputable investing expert? Don't let another day pass without contacting a local SmartVestor Pro to begin making plans for your future!

CHAPTER 4

HOW MUCH DO I NEED TO SAVE FOR A COMFORTABLE RETIREMENT?

How much money should be set aside for retirement and how to go about doing this are two of the most significant problems on many people's minds.

According to George Howard, chartered financial planner at The Fry Group, "Everyone's circumstances are different, depending on when you want to retire, where, and what retirement looks like for you."

The answer to the issue of how much money I need to save for retirement is a crucial component of retirement planning. The answer varies depending on the individual and is mostly influenced by your current salary and the retirement lifestyle you want and can afford.

Even though it's only the first step, knowing how much money you need to save depending on your current age will set you on the right path to achieving your retirement objectives.

The advice of many retirement gurus includes saving 10 times your pre-retirement salary and preparing to live on 80% of your pre-retirement yearly income.

Accordingly, if your annual salary at retirement is $100,000, you'll need at least $80,000 to maintain a good standard of living.

Depending on additional sources of income, including Social Security, pensions, and part-time employment, as well as aspects like your health and chosen lifestyle, this amount may be increased or decreased.

The advice of many retirement gurus includes saving 10 times your pre-retirement salary and preparing to live on 80% of your pre-retirement yearly income.

Accordingly, if your annual salary at retirement is $100,000, you'll need at least $80,000 to maintain a good standard of living.

Depending on additional sources of income, including Social Security, pensions, and part-time employment, as well as aspects like your health and chosen lifestyle, this amount may be increased or decreased.

The save-nothing strategy is obviously not advised. Retirement works best when the stresses of years one through 65 (or so) start to disappear, allowing time for leisure, enjoyment, and grandchildren. However, if money is tight, financial worries may overshadow these pleasures. Want to discover how to enjoy your retirement? begin saving.

On the other hand, it is unreasonable to attempt and save every penny that isn't already allocated for paying bills or purchasing groceries, just as it is bad to save nothing at all.

For the majority of seniors, Social Security is the main source of retirement income outside of savings. The general belief is that Social Security, some savings, and a more frugal lifestyle (no more children at home, no more commuting expenses) will all contribute to financial security in our later years.

In other words, it's a popular belief that if we save in good faith, everything will work out. That might be the case for some people, but success tales like these are more often the consequence of good fortune than of prudent retirement planning. Many of us lose interest at the mention of a "sound retirement strategy" in that sentence. It carries a lot of negative connotations, like high-priced investment advisors, mountains of paperwork, and intricate spreadsheets, to mention a few.

However, a reliable retirement savings strategy doesn't need to be difficult. It all comes down to this one straightforward inquiry: How much do I need to save for retirement? You may eliminate the financial worries that far too many seniors experience by setting aside a portion of your pay each month from now until you retire.

One resource is a retirement calculator. It's crucial to think about the type of lifestyle you want to lead in retirement in order to determine exactly what it will take to retire comfortably. Are you planning to travel? To Paris or somewhere a little more affordable? How frequently would you like to eat out? or visit a theatre? The shore? Do you desire to relocate nearer the beach?

The grandkids? These inquiries might seem insignificant right now, but they can assist you in anticipating the amount of money you'll require in the future. You're going to need a substantial nest fund to draw from if you're determined to see the Taj Mahal, the Pyramids at Giza, and the Eiffel Tower. On the other hand, you won't need to save as much if you anticipate leading a fairly simple life with far fewer expenses than you do now.

A general rule of thumb when thinking about your retirement lifestyle is to replace 70% of your yearly income before retiring. A combination of retirement income sources, such as Social Security, investments, and savings from 401(k)s, IRAs, and other retirement savings accounts, can be planned to achieve this. Important elements like inflation, which will raise prices over time and reduce how much you can buy with your money, must be taken into account as well.

Create a realistic retirement plan; that's what's crucial. Don't undervalue your future self by thinking that canned tuna and scrambled eggs will suffice. In retirement, some expenses will probably decrease independently of inflation, while others might increase. Particularly, medical expenses are likely to increase during retirement. It is therefore best to keep a cushion for unforeseen expenses like that. Additionally, treat yourself well because retirement is your reward for years of arduous effort.

IF YOU ASK THREE FINANCIAL SPECIALISTS HOW MUCH YOU NEED TO SAVE FOR RETIRING, THEIR ANSWERS COULD VARY: A particular amount, like $1 million; a projection of future spending, such as the amount needed to withdraw 80% to 90% of your pre-retirement income annually; or a straightforward calculation, like saving 12 times your pre-retirement pay. What, though, is right for you? How do you know when you're on the right track?

"Because there are so many variables, even the retirement researchers can't agree on a total dollar amount," claims Ben Storey, director of Retirement Research & Insights at Bank of America. The needs of each individual will differ depending on a variety of variables. These variables include your current age, the age at which you intend to retire or may be required to retire due to health issues, the loss of a job, or other uncontrollable circumstances, the expected length of your life based on your family's medical history, the amount you intend to spend during retirement, and the sources of your retirement income.

Fidelity advises that you set aside at least 15% of your pre-tax income for retirement. This belief is not exclusive to Fidelity; the majority of financial counsellors also advocate a similar rate of retirement savings, and research from the Centre for Retirement Research at Boston College supports this recommendation.

However, for many people, saving for retirement is more complicated than just allocating 15% of their income.

The 15% rule of thumb assumes a few things, including that you start saving very early in life. You would need to start saving at age 25 if you wanted to retire by 62, or at age 35 if you wanted to retire by 65, in order to be able to retire comfortably using the 15% guideline.

You should save at least 15% of your pre-tax salary for retirement, according to Fidelity. This viewpoint is not unique to Fidelity; the majority of financial advisors likewise recommend a comparable rate of retirement savings, and findings from the Boston College Centre for Retirement Research support this advice.

However, many people find that saving for retirement involves more than just setting aside 15% of their salary.

A few things, including that you begin saving extremely early in life, are presupposed by the 15% rule of thumb. To be able to retire comfortably using the 15% rule, you would need to start saving at age 25 if you wanted to retire by 62, or at age 35 if you wanted to retire by 65.

HOW TIME AFFECTS RETIREMENT SAVINGS

The most effective ally you have while saving for retirement is time. Small investments made early in your career might grow far more than even significant investments made later in life.

The majority of Americans, let's face it, cannot afford to save a whole 15% of their salary for retirement. But don't let that get you down. Any retirement investment allows you to take advantage of compounding as soon as feasible.

Think about two fictitious investors. A starts making $100 a month in investments when he turns 25. If they received yearly returns of 10%, which is the long-term average return of the S&P 500, they would have a retirement account balance of more than $640,000 by the age of 65.

Investor B started saving when he was 35, but he only put $200 in each month. Despite making about $25,000 more in contributions, Investor B would have nearly $200,000 less in their retirement account at the age of 65.

When analysing investment returns, the difference between Investors A and B demonstrates the importance of time and compounding. Just ten years might have a significant impact on the prospective profits of your assets.

More importantly, it demonstrates that even if you couldn't start investing as early in your life, you may still generate extremely big returns. In the second case, Investor B made only a $72,000 personal investment beginning at the age of 35. They received investment returns of roughly $380,000 as a result.

1. "The 4% Rule"

One simple method, known as the 4% rule, can be used to calculate how much money you will need to save in order to create the required amount of income. It involves dividing your planned annual retirement income by 4%.

You would require a retirement fund of around $2 million ($80,000 /0.04) for an income of $80,000. This plan counts on an investment return of 5% after taxes and inflation, no supplemental retirement income like Social Security, and a standard of living akin to what you would have when you retire.

The 4% rule often predicts that you will retire and live for 30 years. Retirement-age folks need portfolios that can endure longer since they may live longer, and as they age, medical expenditures and other expenses may rise.

2. Savings for Retirement by Age

The key question: "How much do I need to retire?" can be answered by understanding how much you should save for retirement at each stage of your life. On your path to retirement, you can set age-based savings goals using the helpful formulae listed below.

3. Your Salary as a Percentage

It can be helpful to think about saving as a percentage of your wage to determine how much you need to amass at different phases of your life.

Starting in your 20s and continuing throughout your working life, Fidelity Investments advises saving 15% of your gross income. If you have access to a 401(k) or another employer-sponsored plan, this should include any savings you have in various retirement accounts as well as any employer payments you get to those accounts.

4. A Different Formula

Another heuristic calculation states that you should start saving 25% of your annual gross income in your 20s. The 25% savings target may seem intimidating. But keep in mind that it also includes other types of retirement savings, in addition to your employer's matching payments and 401(k) holdings.

This equation should enable you to reach financial independence by the age of 30. If the average savings rate remains constant, the results should be as follows:

Age 35—two times annual salary

Age 40—three times annual salary

Age 45—four times annual salary

Age 50—five times annual salary

Age 55—six times annual salary

Age 60—seven times annual salary

Age 65—eight times annual salary

CHAPTER 5

WHAT'S THE BEST WAY TO PLAN FOR LONG-TERM CARE EXPENSES IN RETIREMENT?

No matter how far away you are from retirement, making future plans is essential for a stable financial situation.

Although the majority of individuals are aware that they must save enough money to pay their basic living expenditures in retirement, many fail to account for other typical - and expensive - costs like medical and long-term care services.

Many seniors need medical services that Medicare doesn't cover, and some have housing and other long-term care needs that they didn't plan for when they were making retirement savings.

The good news is that there are goods and services out there to assist in planning for and managing these costs, such as long-term care insurance, which helps safeguard retirees' assets by covering long-term care services and support in different residential settings, including your own home. It's crucial to take long-term care costs into account while making financial plans and to find solutions that suit your needs.

Many retirees fear outliving their funds as they live longer. The cost of long-term care is an impending expense, yet many elderly Americans haven't made any preparations.

According to Genworth's 2020 Cost of Care Survey, the median cost of a private room in a nursing home was

$105,850, and the yearly cost of in-home care ranged from $53,768 to $54,912.

These prices do, of course, vary by area. In Massachusetts, private room nursing facilities cost a median monthly fee of $13,535 while pensioners in Tennessee paid $7,619, according to Genworth.

The majority of people envision their retirement as a time when they may pursue new interests, travel, and spend time with loved ones. But as we become older, medical difficulties frequently surface, and sadly, many people don't adequately budget for this reality when they make plans for their retirement.

Because many people receive health insurance through their company while they are employed, we don't often consider the expense when making retirement plans. However, with the cost of health care continuing to grow, it's crucial to make plans for how you'll cover these expenses once you stop working.

Some studies recommend that retirees save aside $300,000 or more for health care expenses throughout retirement, a figure that may be beyond the means of many Americans. Here are some tips on how to budget for healthcare expenses in retirement and what you can do right now to avert a major problem in the future.

Here are five actions you can take right away to aid with planning:

1. Locate the currency of today: Locate all of the retirement programmes offered by your employer, including 401(k), 403(b), SEP-IRA, SIMPLE IRA, and pension accounts. Do the same for any non-workplace assets as well, such as an IRA, home equity, individual retirement account, and investments.

2. Estimate your financial situation after retirement: Calculate what the assets might be valued when you retire. This "guesstimate" will provide you with a rough sense of how much money you might have throughout your retirement years.

3. Take future costs into account: Examine your current spending and project how it may change in retirement. Don't only consider rising medical expenditures; consider other expenses that may drop, including clothing. Estimate how these costs may change as a result of inflation between now and retirement.

4. Examine income and outgoings: Look out how your projected retirement income and projected expenses match up. This will demonstrate whether and how much extra you need to save for retirement.

5. Spend your money wisely: Your confidence and financial situation will improve with more savings and less spending. And if your finances are tight, you might think about deferring your Social Security benefits or working longer as your circumstances allow.

CHAPTER 6

WHAT STEPS SHOULD I TAKE TO TRANSITION FROM A SAVING MINDSET TO A SPENDING MINDSET IN RETIREMENT?

Work, earn, spend, and save again. We all become accustomed to this pattern when we are young adults, or often even earlier. When the time comes to break the cycle, if we're fortunate, we're able to amass a sizable sum of money that positions us for a life of rest.

However, for many people, the transition from lengthy commutes and office politics to never-ending relaxation is anything but the eagerly anticipated break that so many of us envision retirement to be. The absence of freedom and entertainment is replaced by monotony and uncertainty, most of which is caused by concern over spending too much money.

We purchased purchases throughout our working years because we knew there would be more money coming in. We don't have the same safety net in retirement. We must have the ability to accept that we are depleting our money, which is a mindset that, for the majority of us, is difficult to adopt. Even people who have a lifetime stream of passive income get terrified when faced with an expanding portfolio and no plan for how to spend it.

These financial worries are frequently closely tied to other retirement difficulties, like the need to fill our leisure time with worthwhile pursuits that give us a sense of purpose. Thus, overcoming any reluctance to spend our hard-earned money entails more than just careful money management. It necessitates a complete mental adjustment.

When it comes to money, the proverb "old habits die hard" is especially relevant. Even when a significant life event necessitates a change in direction, such as retirement, patterns that you've developed over decades might be challenging to alter.

The attitude shift from saving money to spending the money you've stored up is one of the largest and most difficult transitions new retirees must make.

"Now that you have this big cash, you must use it. According to David John, senior strategic policy advisor at the AARP Public Policy Institute, "For some people, it's almost physically painful."

According to studies cited by CNN, many seniors who have funds take considerable measures to avoid using their accounts. They attempt to subsist instead on fixed incomes from sources like Social Security, pensions, or part-time employment. According to a BlackRock survey, the vast majority of retirees still have at least 80% of their savings two decades after retiring. The drawback is that you can be cutting corners when you don't really have to, which results in a reduction in your quality of life. Kyle Newell, a certified financial planner, frequently needs to remind her clients that their hard-earned savings will support a comfortable retirement.

'Now the money is doing the work [so] they don't have to,' I tell them. People tend to benefit from that, Newell said CNN.

Planning how to access retirement funds is necessary to make the switch from a saving to a spending mindset. The 4% rule is one such tactic. According to the Charles Schwab website, you tally up all of your investments and then take 4% of that total out during your first year of retirement. You just modify the dollar amount you withdraw to account for inflation in succeeding years. The goal of the formula is to prevent you from outliving your funds over a protracted retirement.

Although it's not for everyone, it does offer a base upon which to develop.

In addition, you should consider how money affects your life.

"I attempt to find out why [clients] want the money: Is it just for them to have it? Or to employ it as a tool to accomplish your goals and avoid your failures? David Edmisten, CFP, said on CNN. "Much more time needs to be dedicated to considering a purpose for retirement. People who are clear about their goals and objectives claim to be happier.

Establishing a budget and creating a strategy to pay for your expenses is a fantastic first step. For this, you'll need to keep track of your regular expenses like housing, food, utilities, and medical care, as well as your discretionary spending. Next, consider how those costs would alter throughout retirement.

To reduce your monthly rent or mortgage payment, for instance, you can decide to downsize your property. Additionally, you should budget for one-time expenses like a pricey vacation or a brand-new vehicle.

The fixed income you'll receive in retirement, such as Social Security or pension payments, should also be evaluated. The amount you will need to withdraw from your savings each month is equal to the gap between that income and your anticipated expenses.

"You should have 12 to 24 months' worth of cash a year before retiring," advised Edmisten. "We should never have to sell a stock during a recession to cover spending needs when the market is down."

What obstacles come to mind when you consider retirement planning? While making sure you have enough money saved and that you don't run out of money are usual worries, there is another one you could have overlooked: switching from a saving to a spending mindset.

You've probably adopted the practice of saving money as a strategy to ensure your retirement for many years. Maybe you invested with a long-term strategy, made sure your mortgage was paid off or made contributions to a pension. These wholesome routines might have aided you in developing later-life flexibility and security.

But after you retire, your routine isn't the only thing that could alter; your attitude towards money might too. You'll frequently begin to deplete assets rather than accumulate them. You are permitted to use other assets in addition to drawing a pension income. Although you've previously made sacrifices in order to enjoy a pleasant retirement, it may be harder than you think to start using the nest egg you've built.

If you don't change your perspective, even if you have the resources to achieve your goals, your retirement may fall short of your expectations despite your best efforts during your working years to create it.

For years, you've been working and saving in preparation for retirement.

Even though you might be prepared to stop working full-time, the next difficult step is actually allowing yourself to spend your savings since you won't longer be receiving the income that has been paying for your monthly needs up until now.

Most people find it difficult to make the psychological transition from saver to spender, let alone nest egg manager.

"Now that you have this big cash, you must use it. According to David John, a senior strategic policy advisor at the AARP Public Policy Institute, "For some people, it's almost physically painful."

Spending your money, however, is easier said than done, according to John, because of unforeseen circumstances including market performance, life expectancy, and health problems. People may be reluctant to use their savings because they believe that they have enough money to last them their entire lives but that their future is quite unclear.

So I risk hurting myself if I touch that. Studies show that even among retirees with money, many opt to live off stable sources of income instead, such as Social Security, pensions, or earnings from side jobs they take up. According to a Black Rock survey, after 20 years of retirement, the vast majority of pensioners still have at least 80% of their savings.

That's unquestionably due in part to the fact that they experienced one of the longest bull markets in history from 2009 to 2020, which helped restore some of the resources they drained over the years. They also belong to the final generation of workers to get pensions from their employers. However, regardless of their financial situation, most people struggle with the psychological reluctance to use their savings. Inflation, turbulent markets, and a lack of pensions may make life worse for soon-to-be retirees, according to John.

As you think about the best method to convert your retirement assets into dependable income, you also need to deal with misconceptions and attitudes about retirement that could obstruct your plans. For instance, the same stock market that has given you the gains that have enabled you to retire could also turn against you at the last minute.

A correction or bear market when you are working isn't nice, but it's also not a big concern because you are getting paid. You can profit by purchasing stocks at a discount and seeing them increase in value. Additionally, you have time to wait until the market rebounds.

In retirement, none of these statements are accurate. Let's now take a closer look at four tactics that can help you transition smoothly from saving money while you're working to using income from your portfolio in retirement.

1. Eliminate the 4% rule.

The 4% rule is certainly familiar to you, and you might be unconsciously depending on it to provide income in retirement. Recall that the 4% rule or standard that retirees withdraw 4% of their savings year when they are retired to ensure they have enough income to prevent running out of money.

This criterion, which was made popular by financial advisor William Bengen in 1994, is regrettably ineffective for many seniors. In my experience, this regulation would result in many retirees running out of money even if they have additional income sources in addition to savings and Social Security.

This is so because a general approach like the 4% rule doesn't account for market changes and unique retirement goals. It makes sense when you consider it. A few examples of how it could function are shown in Figure 1.

Figure 1: 4% Rule

Retirement Savings	Withdrawal Rate	Annual Income
$500,000	4%	$20,000
$750,000	4%	$30,000
$1,000,000	4%	$40,000

The 4% rule counts on the market remaining steady for the duration of retirement. There is no chance that will occur.

Think about the market's potential devastation if you had retired in 2007 while adhering to the 4% guideline, as shown in Figure 2. This analysis is based on a $ 500,000 investment in the S&P 500 from 2007 to 2011.

Figure 2: Example of 4% withdrawal rate from 2005 to 2010

Year	Retirement Savings	Market Return	Annual Income
2007	$500,000	5.49%	$20,000.00

Year	Retirement Savings	Market Return	Annual Income
2008	$527,450	-37.00%	$21,098.00
2009	$332,293.50	26.48%	$13,291.74
2010	$420,284.81	15.08%	$16,811.40
2011	$483,663.76	2.11%	$19,346.55

In a weak market, the drawbacks of this approach are obvious. First of all, it is difficult, if not impossible, to know for sure that you will be able to pay all of your debts because you cannot rely on a specific amount of money each year.

Second, it takes a while for your portfolio to recover after suffering a loss during a bad market. And because you still need to withdraw money from it, this further depletes the principal.

"Endowment Method" is a different rule. With this more flexible method, you can move your retirement income up or down to reflect gains or losses by withdrawing 3% to 5% of the value of your portfolio each year. Your income will fluctuate based on the account's market performance.

2. Reevaluate your risk tolerance.

As I said, when you have a job and a regular paycheck, it's simple to have a high-risk tolerance. Since time is on your side, you can weather any market turbulence. You may even profit from it if you are purchasing assets at a discount and reaping the rewards of their appreciation.

In contrast, the reverse occurs in retirement, and it can be disastrous. If you have a large portion of your assets significantly invested in the market, you will always need to take money out to cover expenses. If that occurs during a protracted down market, it can make it harder for you to draw income from your investments for the remainder of your retirement.

Re-evaluating your risk tolerance as you approach retirement and setting up your assets for distribution is the best course of action in this situation. Realising that you need to be more careful in retirement since your money must last for an undetermined amount of years is only prudent.

My general rule of thumb is to deduct your age from 100 to determine how much should be kept invested in the stock market. That would entail retaining 35% of your assets in the stock market if you are 65. That gives you stock market exposure without jeopardising your retirement distribution plan in the event of a protracted downturn.

3: Take into account assured income techniques

Using guaranteed income solutions as a component of a retirement distribution plan can offer stability. One of the products I employ in retirement portfolios is a fixed index annuity since it offers guaranteed income* and allows access to the principal for withdrawals if necessary. Annuities aren't liquid assets, of course, as they may have high surrender fees.

To get your money back if you need it during the early phases of an annuity contract, you must pay a surrender charge that might be as high as 10% after you purchase an annuity.

By investing a portion of your investment in an annuity, you can shield those funds from market fluctuations and provide a steady income stream for the duration of your retirement.

Depending on how much you contribute, the insurance company that issues the annuity assumes the risk of investing the money in exchange for you receiving a specific amount of monthly income.

4: Design a distribution strategy

A retirement account is not a retirement plan, as I have already stated, and it is surely not a plan for retirement distributions. A retirement distribution plan considers your investments from the standpoint of the income required to maintain your retirement lifestyle, as well as other sources of income.

Let's imagine you and your spouse have $750,000 in retirement assets, $4,500 in Social Security benefits per month, and a $1,000 monthly pension. If your monthly income requirement is $8,500 (adjusted for inflation), you will need to bring in $3,000 from your investment portfolio each month to make up the difference between your current monthly income of $5,500 from Social Security and pension benefits and your monthly income requirement.

Then, using $375,000 of your retirement assets, you might buy an annuity that would pay out $1,500 each month, or half of what you require. The remaining retirement funds might then be put into a mix of bonds and stocks that would provide both growth and income.

In that case, you would require $18,000 in withdrawals annually to meet your residual income requirement of $1,500 per month. Because you built a three-legged stool and diversified your portfolio between risky assets like stocks and bonds and assets that deliver guaranteed income, that is far more feasible and less dangerous.

Making a distribution plan that balances your income needs with the real income you can dependably and securely draw from your portfolio will put you in a position to enjoy your retirement without having to worry about running out of money.

YOUR RETIREMENT MINDSET HAS TO CHANGE

1. RECOGNISE YOUR EMOTIONS

There is no right or incorrect way to react to such a momentous transition in one's life as retirement. Allow yourself the time and space to experience your feelings without trying to force yourself to feel a certain way about your retirement, regardless of how you're feeling about your working life—whether you're anxious or sad about it. You'll realise that any unfavourable feelings will disappear with time.

2. ADOPT A NEW ATTITUDE

Sometimes all it takes is a small change in perspective to relieve the stress associated with using your retirement savings. Think of your spending as a gain as opposed to a loss. After years of having to forego wonderful experiences for a day at work, you can now make up for those lost chances, whether they were lavish international holidays or priceless time spent with friends and family.

3, SEEK NEW SUCCESS

Giving up all of your motivation does not imply switching to a life of ease. It entails shifting the focus of all that energy. Along with helping you avoid the boredom that so many retirees fear, setting and achieving new goals helps you to reevaluate your sense of self and discover who you are apart from your job title.

4. IMPROVE YOUR SOCIAL NETWORKS

Spending your days in a busy office makes it simple to satisfy your fundamental need for human connection. Even those with more lonely jobs have probably formed contacts that are directly related to their line of work. When these social links are severed, the effect can be upsetting.

Make it a point to develop social connections, whether that involves staying in touch with former coworkers, joining a support group, signing up for a retirement transition programme, or doing all of the above, in order to strengthen your coping abilities and enhance your quality of life overall.

5. NEVER FORGET THAT RETIREMENT IS NOT ALL OR NOTHING

You should be able to reap the rewards of your years of hard work, but retirement shouldn't be an opportunity for reckless spending. To put it another way, leveraging your assets doesn't necessarily include taking a fancy vacation, for instance.

Sometimes it simply entails spending a little bit more on that work of art you've had your eye on. You'll ultimately acquire a sense of how you can live happily and comfortably within the retirement budget you've established for yourself if you find the things that make you happy, take it easy, try different things out, and so on.

ASK A FINANCIAL PLANNER FOR ADVICE

A qualified viewpoint can significantly reduce anxiety. A financial advisor (preferably one who specialises in retirement planning) has the knowledge to put you on the proper path towards a guilt-free life of leisure, whether retirement is still a long-term goal or is just around the horizon.

In addition, your financial situation doesn't stop if you quit your full-time employment. You still need to make important financial decisions in retirement, from health insurance to estate planning, and everything in between. You may get the financial guidance you need to make such decisions carefully from a dependable counsellor.

CHAPTER 7

HOW CAN I LEAVE A LEGACY FOR MY LOVED ONES WHILE ENSURING MY OWN FINANCIAL SECURITY IN RETIREMENT?

For many of us, it's crucial to leave a lasting legacy for the people and causes that are most important to us. It is possible to leave a financial legacy that will help your heirs, your church, or the causes you care about after you pass away with careful planning and execution.

We'll talk about how you can create a lasting impression with your gift and leave a legacy. People frequently begin thinking about legacy planning as they get closer to retirement, including how they'll be remembered and what they'll leave behind. In most situations, it takes careful planning and the guidance of a financial advisor to leave a legacy for children, grandkids, or charities — or other causes people are passionate about.

Even though it's sometimes disregarded, legacy planning may be a difficult but effective undertaking with significant advantages for both individuals and families. Long-term financial choices are part of leaving the world a better place, in addition to more obvious achievements like great works of art or charitable giving.

Your legacy plan is focused on creating the standards and procedures that will help you thoughtfully transfer your wealth, including your property, mementoes, and assets, from one generation to the next. It lets you secure your possessions, make sure your loved ones are financially taken care of, and transmit valuable knowledge about how money works and should be managed.

Decide what you want your financial legacy to be.

Establishing your mission and thinking about how you want to utilise your donations to support your heirs and community should be your first steps. If you have investigated your aims, goals, and motives, it will be simpler to develop a plan of action. By being proactive now, you can subsequently support your loved ones.

In order to save your family from incurring expenses, ask yourself:

• Have you financially paid for funeral arrangements?

• Are there any additional household expenses you want to make sure are met after your departure?

•Will it have an impact on how your spouse finances their retirement?

• How will you make sure that your family's traditions are upheld?

• Do you have the money set aside to cover your children's or grandchildren's future educational costs?

•What causes are most important to you, and what legacy do you hope to leave?

•How do you currently support your church, if you're an active churchgoer?

Leaving a financial legacy

Make a list of the ways your financial legacy might be used to help others. There are numerous ways to donate now and in the afterlife. Take into account whatever you have to impart:

Your time, abilities, or knowledge

Stocks, mutual funds, and other assets;

Retirement accounts like IRAs or 401(k)s;

Annuities or life insurance policies

Your home or other property

A business you control

A nonprofit foundation you formed

With the guidance of a financial advisor and estate planning lawyer, you may assess your alternatives and assets and determine which plans are the most appropriate for your objectives and circumstances.

Thrivent can work with you and your tax expert or attorney, even though we do not offer specialised legal or tax advice.

Six things to think about when leaving a financial legacy

Create a plan that makes the most of financial instruments designed for generosity and giving to operate in concert with the legacy you want to leave your descendants in order to solidify your legacy. Here are some typical approaches that individuals use:

a. Verify that your beneficiary designations are current by:

Beneficiary designations are an easy method to spell out your financial legacy. When you designate a person or group as the beneficiary of a financial account, contract, or insurance policy, the asset can be transferred to them after your passing—typically without the hassle or cost of probate. A key component of your estate plan that can streamline the estate settlement process is the designation of beneficiaries.

b. Make a charitable trust that will benefit both your heirs and the cause

A financial legacy can be arranged through charitable trusts. For instance, charitable remainder trusts enable you to continue receiving income from the assets trust while you are still alive, with the remaining assets going to the charity of your choice.

While charitable lead trusts allow you to bequeath the assets to a beneficiary other than a charity, such as your children, they also allow a charity to receive income while you are alive.

c. Use a charitable gift annuity to receive a stream of income while you're still alive.

Similar to generous remainder trusts are charitable gift annuities. You donate assets to a charity, and the charity invests them and pays you an income for the rest of your life. After your death, the charity keeps the donation while the income payments stop.

d. Make a donor-advised fund that is unique to you.

Donor-advised funds enable you to deduct charitable contributions from your income and invest the proceeds and direct gifts over time in accordance with your preferences. Since the assets can continue to grow and be used to fund gifts even after your death, donor-advised funds are especially helpful for involving several generations of your family in a culture of giving.

e. Put others first by purchasing life insurance

Whether you want to leave money to loved ones, close friends, or a charity that means a lot to you, life insurance contracts can be an affordable method to do so. A life insurance payout can be an effective way to transfer wealth because, for the most part, the receiver doesn't have to pay taxes on the death benefit.

f. In your will, specify the receivers of gifts.

Your will is a useful instrument for both expressing your wishes to your family and for charitable giving. Making sure your objectives are clearly stated in your will and including provisions for both your family and gifts may also assist you in avoiding having to pay estate taxes.

AREAS WHERE PEOPLE CAN LEAVE A LEGACY

Vacation Homes Make a Great Inheritance: One big area where people can leave a legacy is real estate, such as a second home or a vacation property. "Sometimes families have a vacation home that means a lot to the family," says certified financial planner Constance Stone, co-founder and consultant to Ohio-based Stepping Stone Financial, Inc.

However individuals interested in doing so should explore setting up a family limited partnership or a trust for an easier process to transfer interest in the property.

According to Stone, leaving behind a vacation home "can be a wonderful thing—and also a source of disagreement and problems. You have to think ahead of how to set it up so that the entity keeps going." There are also some tax breaks for family limited partnerships in addition to the ability to transfer ownership between different siblings, Stone adds.

Be Clear About Your Family Home and Personal Belongings: While vacation real estate can be a slam dunk for an inheritance, the same isn't always true of the family home.

"The family home can be tough because it's fraught with so much emotion," says Stone. "I've seen more family conflict over the family home and its contents than anything else."

People thinking about leaving collectables or anything worth monetary or sentimental value should include directions in estate planning documents with clear instructions for how those items are to be divided.

"Leave a list: If you want to leave certain things to certain family members, that list will generally be honoured, as long as it's referenced in the will," Stone says.

Create a Beneficiary IRA: Another way to leave a lasting legacy is by naming children or grandchildren as the beneficiaries of traditional Individual Retirement Accounts (IRAs) or Roth IRAs. "The best thing you can leave to children are Roth IRAs," says Stone, noting the tax expense of traditional IRAs.

Distributions from Roth IRAs are tax-free as long as the person who set it up met the five-year holding period for contributions and conversions, she notes. Beneficiaries have five years to take out money from the account unless they transfer the retirement plan account to an Inherited IRA, which allows them to stretch distributions throughout their life expectancy.

"If you don't convert it to an Inherited IRA [after the donor dies], then you have to take [all the money in the account] in five years," says certified financial planner Karen DeRose, founder of Illinois-based DeRose Financial Planning Group, of both traditional and Roth accounts.

People choosing to set up beneficiary IRAs can name multiple beneficiaries, Stone says. Once the donor dies, the IRA is divided into separate accounts for each beneficiary and they can access their funds independently of the other beneficiaries.

While there is no legal limit to the number of beneficiaries that can be named on an IRA, some institutions limit that number.

To make sure IRAs are set up correctly to avoid distribution penalties or taxes, it's best to talk to a knowledgeable tax advisor, as DeRose and Stone recommend.

Name a Child as Beneficiary for an Annuity: Similar to beneficiary IRAs, it's also possible to purchase an annuity and name a child as the beneficiary. Upon the donor's death, the child then has an income stream from annuity payments over their lifetime. "Because the child is younger, there will be a bigger stream of income throughout their lifetime," says DeRose. "It's another great way to guarantee a child's income."

Use Excess Distributions for a Second-to-Death Life Insurance Policy: Prior to 2019, when individuals reached age 70 ½, they were required to start taking required minimum distributions (RMDs) from qualified retirement plans, such as Individual Retirement Accounts (IRAs) and 401(k)s (excluding a current 401(k) if the individual is still working).

However, the SECURE Act passed in 2019, made a big change to RMD requirements by extending the age from 70½ to 72. Distributions start at a certain percentage of the total balance of all IRAs and increase as the individual gets older.

"A lot of people don't need the money [from the required distributions] and turn around and reinvest it," DeRose says of her clients. "If you don't need it, I tell them, 'Why don't you take part of it and buy a second-to-die life insurance policy?'"

These policies pay out only after the second spouse in a couple passes away, making it one of the cheaper life insurance policies, according to DeRose. As an example, suppose there is a married couple with two children that purchases a $1 million second-to-die policy that costs between $20,000 and 25,000 a year and they pay for it with their excess distributions.

Once both spouses pass away, their two children each get $500,000 from the policy. "Putting the insurance payout into an irrevocable trust makes it income- and estate tax-free, and they're leveraging their gifting," DeRose adds. "It's a beautiful thing to do. It's a great strategy."

Gift Depreciating Stock to Charities; For those desiring to leave behind a legacy benefiting a charity they're passionate about, a Roth IRA may not be a good idea because non-profit, 501(c)3 organizations don't benefit from tax breaks like individuals do, says Stone.

However, bequesting depreciated stock to a charity can lower estate taxes. "If you had a lot of stock that depreciated in value that you want to unload, those are often looked at for charities," she advises.

"It gets the depreciated stock out of your estate, and you don't have to pay taxes on that—and the charity isn't impacted by taxes either."

Leaving a legacy isn't all about the money, either, adds Stone, who advocates for a more holistic view. For example, many people don't think about cleaning out their homes while they're still around to do it. "Get rid of the stuff you don't want to be left behind, so someone else doesn't have to make those hard choices," she says.

"Kids feel like they're throwing their parents' lives away. If they're already going through an emotional time, it makes it even harder. There's a sense of guilt." Another lasting legacy is in the form of lifestyle.

"Some of the best things that my parents left me were an appreciation for what I had, and not expecting—or wanting—a lot of material things," Stone says. "Family was important. Religion and church were important. Hard work was expected, and it helped me develop good life skills."

Putting your legacy plan into action: Deciding which tactics to implement for your planned giving goals is a big step that you can approach in stages. First think about your ideals, your values and the legacy you want to leave.

When you have this in mind, then you can map out the details of setting your legacy on course. Weigh which strategies might be best suited for your goals and start putting them in motion. If you need guidance along the way, Thrivent financial advisors have the expertise to help you with your plans.

CONCLUSION

Readers set off on a road to a happy and secure retirement when they read "The success code for your dream retirement". This thorough manual provides a road map for organising and navigating this thrilling stage of life. This book addresses the key elements of retirement planning, from financial knowledge and investment techniques to health and lifestyle decisions. Learn how to make the most of your retirement money, design a satisfying life after work, keep your health, and leave a lasting legacy for your loved ones. "The success code for your dream retirement" is your go-to resource for making the most of your senior years. It offers insightful guidance and practical suggestions to support you in living the retirement of your dreams.

The fundamental insight that true retirement success goes much beyond financial matters is at the core of this book. "The Success Code for Your Dream Retirement" analyses the many facets of retirement preparation and offers a comprehensive approach that addresses both the quantitative and qualitative parts of this journey, even if cautious financial planning is unquestionably essential.

This book offers helpful suggestions, helpful hints, and inspirational anecdotes that will appeal to readers of all backgrounds and ages by drawing on a plethora of research, professional interviews, and real-life events. It is a flexible tool that can be customised to suit unique needs and goals, making it useful for both people who are just starting to plan for retirement and those who are currently making use of their retirement years.

The book "The Success Code for Your Dream Retirement" is more than just a guide to a future full of opportunity. It gives readers the ability to picture their own special retirement aspirations and provides them with the tools necessary to make those aspirations a colourful reality. You'll learn as you immerse yourself in its pages that retirement isn't the end of the road but rather the start of a brand-new, thrilling chapter in your life's journey.